21 Breaths

—

First published by Unify,
an imprint of Unicorn Publishing Group LLP, 2021
5 Newburgh Street
London W1F 7RG
www.unicornpublishing.org

ISBN 978-1-913491-47-5
10 9 8 7 6 5 4 3 2 1

Designed by Katie Greenwood
Cover designed by Felicity Price-Smith
Printed in Europe by Fine Tone Ltd

21 Breaths

BREATHING TECHNIQUES
TO CHANGE YOUR LIFE

OLIVER JAMES

UNIFY

Thank you, Samuel.

Without you, the words and gifts of this book would, without doubt, have remained but the colours and sounds of my dreams.

Let us each take a moment just to breathe.

A breath to connect with ourselves.

A breath to connect with others.

A breath to connect with the
world under our feet.

As gentle as a raindrop and
as powerful as an ocean.

Breath is always there.

Like stepping stones
waiting to be discovered.

The frontier between what we
know and what we can only imagine.

A magnetic north and pathway home.

A pathway back to ourselves.

CONTENTS

The 21 Breaths

Re-Discovering Breath

Breath is easy to take for granted. For many, breathing happens so effortlessly; so unconsciously, that we forget it takes place at all. Breathing techniques are powerful in this respect: they bring presence to a magnificence that would otherwise remain hidden and awaken a potential that would, otherwise, stay asleep.

When I hear someone say: "Breathing techniques? Oh... no thank you. They are not for me!" I find myself smiling on the inside. I imagine these people have an image of what it means to practise breath: perhaps they see someone high up on a mountain with closed eyes and folded legs; a look of composure and serenity; an image that could not be further from the truth.

Those new to breathing techniques are often surprised to learn they have been engaging them all their lives. Long before we draw our first, truly conscious breath, our body has already spent a lifetime in practice: when we yawn; when we sigh; when we hold our breath or hyperventilate from exercise. All of these are breathing techniques: our body has purposefully changed the rate and depth of respiration and has been doing so from the moment we took our very first breath!

Though breathing techniques can easily appear foreign and unknown to us, it would be more accurate to describe the process of using them as respiring towards an increasingly familiar landscape. Since our body is already committed to the task, why not join in; why not help ourselves along?

It is from this place that the seeds of *21 Breaths* was inspired. Rather than aiming to encourage a discovery of breathing techniques, this book sets out to support a re-discovery and reconnection; to reawaken the immeasurable wisdom that awaits us all at the misty edges of our breath.

There is an indescribable quality here. In this moment, the unfamiliar becomes familiar and, merging with the infinite capabilities of breath, it becomes forever part of who we are.

I wish you all the best in your own re-discovery of breath.

An Unexpected Introduction

─────

"Sounds very interesting," says the man opposite me. Noticing his eyes glaze over, it feels safe to assume the conversation between us has been anything but interesting.

This is Tim. Having met only ten minutes ago at a friend's birthday dinner, I notice he is desperately looking around for someone to come and save him. I do not mind. This often happens when I get over-excited about breath. Breath and breathing techniques have long been a beautiful madness of mine. To be fair, he was the one that got me started. Should someone show even the slightest interest in breath, too easily do I leap into a conversation about its potential miracles. I am certain everyone would if they knew what was possible.

Another few minutes of awkwardness pass. I notice Tim's face has changed from mild helplessness to intense focus; it seems to me like he is working out how to excuse himself from the table.

"If only I had sat there!" I imagine him to be thinking, as he gazes at chairs further down the table. I feel my breath catch on the uneasiness. Actually, I quite enjoy these clumsy moments. They are an opportunity to practise what I am always encouraging others to do: to breathe into whatever arises and stay present in the face of discomfort. Bolstered by this reminder, my own breath noticeably deepens. It is almost exciting watching myself return to balance simply from breathing.

To recapture Tim's interest, I decide to share a breathing technique with him. Now really... who wouldn't be fascinated to learn there is a breath for everything? My mind races to decide which will most effectively reveal breath's wonder.

Okay! There are the essentials: the techniques that could help Tim have an amazing night's sleep, unwind from stress or improve his posture; or maybe we should talk about more specialist practice: breaths to help improve his fitness or alleviate health concerns such as asthma and high blood pressure. Oh... but wait! What about the life-transforming techniques: the ones that relieve pain, clear anxiety or induce a whole-body orgasm?

"Stop!" roars a voice in my mind. Noticing my breath has stalled once again, it is clear I am still trying too hard. As it returns, relaxed and slow, I am reminded of something important; something we all come to learn about this extraordinary, life-essential process. Breath is meaningless without connection; just movements of air pulled in and out of our atmosphere. A breath must be felt for it to touch a heart.

I decide to hold my next breath deep in my lungs. I find this helps to slow me down. Quickly, I notice everything turns quiet. Where there had been such urgency to share some amazing breath-related insight with Tim now only felt peaceful and still. "What is this sensation?" I enquired within. It was trust.

I could trust that everything was as it was meant to be. Perhaps my excitement had been a little intense for Tim but, somehow, this had been necessary. Giving breath a voice always feels sacred in this respect, like planting a seed in the earth. An image of a sapling sprouting from the soil and spreading

itself into a humongous, deeply rooted tree plays in my mind. Everything goes quiet again. It is as though a breeze has brushed my cheeks and rustled the imaginary leaves that tower over my head. Something is coming. I can feel it. In anticipation, my spine begins to tingle and then words I once heard materialise out of nothing behind my eyes: from little acorns do mighty oaks grow.

Feeling the excitement of it all, I find myself taking a sharp breath in and holding onto it, tightly. As I let my breath go, I feel I can let the whole topic of breathing go with it. It does not take long for Tim's startled eyes to soften and for him to finally settle at the table. I think changing the topic to bees helped. It turns out these pollinating wonders are his favourite! Tactfully, I manage to steer clear from discussing how they breathe. What a shame. There is something otherworldly about their pore-like spiracles and muscleless airflow.

A little later, while waiting for dessert, I see Tim's face wince sharply. I notice it happens again; and again. Feeling concern, I check if he is okay. Taking a large, chest-billowing inhale, Tim unleashes into an impassioned story about the belly cramps he gets during almost every mealtime. He vividly describes the varying degrees of pain that impact him after he eats, and the small comfort that he feels knowing doctors have been unable to find anything wrong with him. "It has been a few years this way," he says before another excruciating jolt takes him over.

Of course, this is unfortunate for Tim, but would it be wrong to say I felt that rush of excitement build up inside me once again? Like a bubble about to breach the surface, a familiar voice was desperate to be heard: "I know a breath that could help!"

Fortunately, I seize this notorious catchphrase before it has a chance to escape but the whole keeping-it-in thing does give me bellyache. Feeling my stomach turn into knots, it is clear my whole being is trying to protect Tim from another onslaught of breath-related madness.

"Is there a breath that could help?" he asks for himself, before feigning embarrassment and throwing his head into his hands. Not wanting to scare him off, I remain composed but as you might imagine, inside, fireworks are going off.

Within ten minutes, Tim is perched on a bar stool, his back resting up against a wall. The scene has attracted a large group of people from our table including Aisha, the lady whose birthday it is. Despite the amused chatter surrounding us, Tim remains surprisingly focused. His body appears free from discomfort and continues to enjoy the breath offered to him.

"You are the last person in the world I would expect to be doing this sort of thing!" Aisha chuckles at Tim. The crowd giggle with her. A part of me expected him to sit bolt upright but he remains still and breathing. Only a smile beams on his face.

It is when the scene blurs that I realise just how moved I am. How could I not be? Out of the two hundred and sixty-three million breaths that Tim has ever taken, I had just witnessed the connecting breath; that magical moment when a breath is breathed that changes every breath ever after. It always feels such an honour to bear witness to these moments. And, every time it happens, I am reminded why I get so excited about breath.

Because I know it only takes a moment for a breath to touch a heart.

The Moment Breath Changed My Life

I remember it well, the moment that breath changed my life. The time was 11:46am on Saturday, 21st May 2016.

It feels important to say that, before this extraordinary Saturday, breath had already played a huge and pivotal role in my life. How could it not? As a body-led psychotherapist and Pilates teacher with over sixteen years' experience, it is safe to say breath and breathing techniques had already proven their boundless ability to offer support in one form or another; but, before this extraordinary Saturday, breath had yet to change my life.

At 11:46am on Saturday, 21st May 2016, I was standing in front of three examiners in Nijmegen, Holland. For the last ten minutes, they had been asking questions about the case study session I had just completed, live, for my psychotherapy certification. It was Anna Timmermans, one of Europe's most prominent body-led psychotherapists, who asked the final question. I remember feeling a hint of nervousness as she took a breath to speak. She had a way of asking questions that pierce through the heart of any matter.

"Why did you choose your intervention?" she asked, referencing my use of a breathing technique. It was a good question. With the countless methods and techniques I could have chosen, why breath? Quicker than my mind had time to ponder, words poured from my mouth that, to this day, still cover me in goose bumps.

"Everything is in the breath."
came my reply.

These words were as much a surprise to me as to anyone else that morning. Even now, I swear they were not mine. It was as if they had been channelled from another world. The sentence felt to strike deep in my core and pulled me, like a magnet, into its embrace. Then, the most remarkable thing happened.

I am quite certain no one noticed but, beginning in my toes, I felt a wave run through my body; a whooshing sensation that touched every part of me, leaving it humming and vibrating.

As the wave converged up into my head, a pleasant, dizzying sensation started to build before the room turned brilliant white. Everything tremored, for a moment, before my mind seemed to explode into a million shiny pieces.

All around me were fragments of moving images, flashing, and twinkling. They appeared chaotic and jumbled at first but, slowly, their chaos took form and I noticed recognisable moments from my life playing like movies projected onto a magnificent, splintered screen; excitement and joy melted into jealousy and anger; my life's sensuality flowed into my life's grief and fury. Memory after memory played out before each found its place and order. Perhaps I had thought of everything in my life as separate, unique moments, but now, as I stared at their constellation, I sensed a deeper truth: that everything was undeniably connected.

An undulating, silvery thread could be seen running through the shapes and patterns that surrounded me.
I knew in an instant:
the thread was breath.

It is difficult to say how long I stood staring at this beautiful scene but as the room of examiners and colleagues came back into view, I felt those words still hovering in the air. My first awareness was that of curiosity; dark lids rose and fell like curtains before I realised, I was blinking. I noticed my body next; it felt different. A new frequency seemed to pulse through me like an electric current. It felt surreal, to begin with; like we can feel hot and cold or see light and dark, my whole being seemed able to sense breath!

It started as a familiar sensation. Like an old friend, I could feel my own breath as it moved in and out. In and out. Next, I could feel the breath of others in the room. Our breaths were talking to each other, exchanging information and insight. My awareness kept expanding. Hundreds of breathers turned into thousands. Thousands into millions. Soon, it was as though I could feel the whole of Holland breathing. What started as my lone breath now felt like a behemoth of breathing sensation. At the moment when I felt the whole world breathe, a cacophony that was sure to blow me apart, something extraordinary happened: everyone's breath merged into one.

One big breath.
One big breath in. One big breath out.

This experience may sound horrifying, though it was anything but. It was as if the story of everyone's breath played all at once. A story of confinement and freedom; a story of love and pain; a story of humiliation and faith. Everyone's story was present. I would have burst into tears for the immense grief set to overwhelm me, but joy and hope breathed in this space too. It was, quite frankly, incredible.

As I returned to my own body and my own breath, I knew life, or my experience of life, would never be the same again.

Within days of arriving back to London, it felt impossible to continue the way I had. I sold my flat of fifteen years, ended contracts with employers and moved out of the city. From an outsider's perspective, I recognise this might seem extreme but, in truth, it did not feel this way. I felt only relief; like I could breathe for the first time in my life. Of course, I was sad to leave amazing friends and clients; many tears were shed over the months that followed but alongside the sadness was, also, a deep sense of trust.

Every moment had been a transition towards this moment. Every breath had led, one after the other, to the life I was breathing now.

I am not going to lie. To begin with, it was strange! After the weekend in Holland, it felt like I had sensed everything there was to sense about breath and yet I also felt like I knew nothing at all. I knew breath's essence and signature but not its definition or explanation. Reflecting on this time, I realise now that I had

yet to develop a language to speak about it; I could feel breath but perhaps I was yet to be able to describe exactly what it was that I felt.

Quite naturally, I began dedicating time to practise breathing. Starting with just a few minutes each day, engagement developed into hundred-hour weeks spent breathing. Just breathing.

I call this period my Days of Breath. It is an amusing title, with hindsight. Each of us spends every living day breathing but there is something profound in the contrast between breathing consciously and the state of unconscious breathing that most of us are used to. For months, I observed. Practised. Reflected. Experimented. It was during this time that I felt inspired to buy as many books about breathing as I could. Interestingly, these stayed on the shelves beside my bed for at least a few years before being opened. It seemed important they were there. Reassuring, somehow, to have other people's connection to breath close by my side.

Coming out of this prolonged period of breathing in December 2017, I felt ready to connect with others. Setting off around the world, I started interviewing people who worked with breath, from yoga practitioners and meditation specialists to breathworkers, fighter pilots and surgeons. I also sought out as many schools of breath as I could: Holotropic Breath; Transformational Breath; Quantum Light Breath; Shamanic Breath; Wim Hof Method. To this day, this list continues to expand. I love watching it grow and exploring its ever-expanding landscape.

I believe that what stands out for anyone who spends time with all of these breathing disciplines and ideologies is that, underlying their differences, there is something profoundly familiar. I came to learn that the movements and techniques that presented themselves during my own days of breathing were fragments of all the others: extremes of movement and intensity could be found in Kundalini Yoga; the breaths that seemed to change my whole nervous system waited for me in Wim Hof's work; the breaths of joy and acceptance fluttered in Transformational Breath. What more could I have expected?

Even to this day, I notice their connection: that silvery thread tracing through them all.

I look back on this magical period with immense gratitude and awe. It was a wondrous time, rich with insight and adventure. Everyone gave so generously, from the practitioners, specialists and healers to friends and family who opened their hearts and homes to me across the globe. Everyone shared so graciously and, in their own way, contributed to this book.

I hope you enjoy practising *21 Breaths* as much as I have enjoyed writing it. Whether you choose to practise only one breath or feast on all twenty-one, you will find something revealing in every moment's practice: the wonder that comes from discovering your own connection to breath and the beautiful tapestry that unfurls before you, made from that wondrous silvery thread.

How Breathing Techniques Work

───

There is a breath for everything. This might sound like an extraordinary claim, but the reasoning is based on something extraordinarily simple: our entire being, from our physical presence to our thoughts and emotions, are inextricably and completely connected to breath. To understand just how deep the interconnection runs, and why breathing techniques work, it is helpful to consider the workings of our respiratory system in relation to every other system of the body.

RESPIRATORY SYSTEM

A complex and beautifully designed system capable of exchanging huge quantities of essential gas with the outside world. This system is armed with powerful technology ensuring the air we breathe is hydrated, warmed, filtered, cleaned and distributed evenly across the surface of our lungs. Breathing techniques can be used to create a safer breathing environment, improve respiratory function and efficiency while also impacting memory, emotions and learning.

---

1. **OLFACTORY BULB:** Part of the neural structure that helps us to smell. Signals are sent to the brain which, in turn, integrates them with emotion, memory and learning.

2. **NASAL TURBINATES:** Shell-shaped network of bones, vessels and tissue responsible for warming, humidifying and filtering the air we breathe. Nasal hair, mucus and a complex network of blood capillaries cover its surface and help the turbinates to perform their role. They all work together to alter airflow and fight potential infection.

3. **ADENOIDS AND TONSILS:** Tissues that help to trap and kill germs.

4. **EPIGLOTTIS AND GLOTTIS:** Structures that prevent food and large particles entering the windpipe and lungs.

5. **TRACHEA:** Cartilaginous pipe that transports air from the upper respiratory tract to the bronchi. Functioning like circular scaffolding, it prevents airway collapse and humidifies air. Small, hair like structures called cilia line its surface and help transport germ and particle-laden liquid and mucus out of our airways.

6. **LUNGS:** Pair of spongy, air-filled organs located within the rib cage.

7. **BRONCHI:** Two main branches, left and right, channel air into the lungs. Lined with soft tissue, they are believed to humidify air, enhance our voice and offer immunological support.

8. **BRONCHIOLES:** Smaller passages that branch off the bronchi and deliver air to over three hundred million alveoli. Alveoli are the microscopic balloon-like sacs where essential gas exchange takes place between the atmosphere and our blood.

9. **DIAPHRAGM:** Thin, dome shaped muscle responsible for efficient breathing.

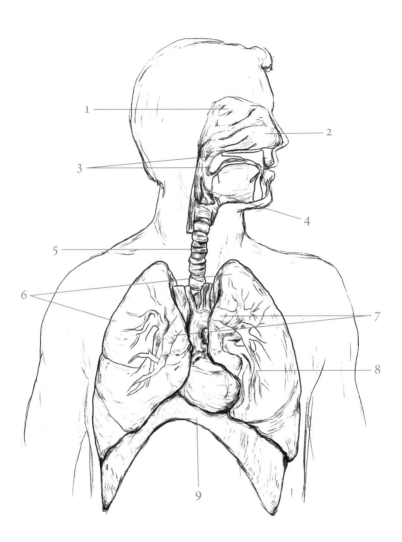

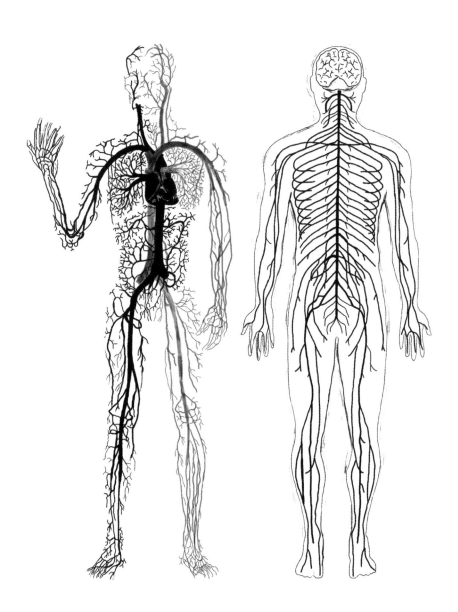

CIRCULATORY SYSTEM

The heart and lungs
work together from our first breath
to our last. Efficient and healthy
breathing can take pressure off
the heart and help circulation
by improving carbon dioxide
and oxygen exchange and cell
respiration. Breathing techniques
can develop fitness, enhance
our metabolism, improve waste
clearance, and increase longevity.

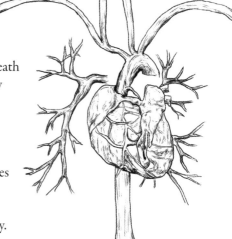

NERVOUS SYSTEM

A complex network of nerves and control centres that function both independently and interdependently to help us to breathe. From a simplistic point of view, important distinctions can be made between the sympathetic nervous system, which is designed to help us survive intense, stressful situations, and the parasympathetic nervous system, which helps us to digest and heal. Breathing techniques can support the complete spectrum covered by the entire nervous system, both enhancing stress resilience while also promoting rest and recuperation.

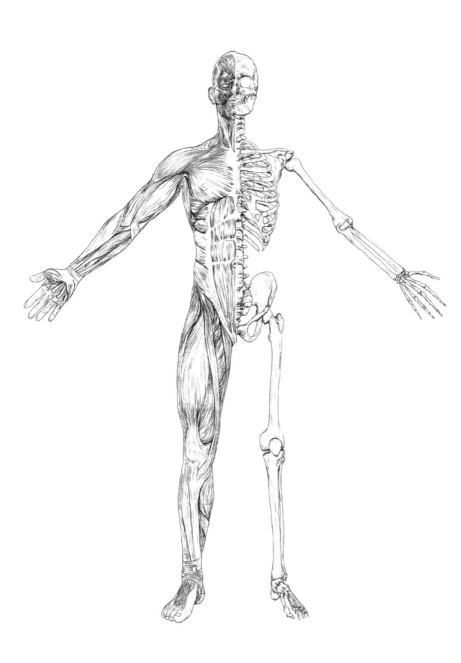

MUSCULOSKELETAL SYSTEM

Muscles and bones depend on the efficient exchange of oxygen and carbon dioxide as much as breathing requires an efficient musculoskeletal system. Their interconnection is most noticeable during exercise and in their decline through ageing. Breathing techniques can improve musculoskeletal efficiency while boosting fitness, strength, and longevity.

LYMPHATIC SYSTEM

A key part of our immunological defence that plays a huge role in both our body's protection and internal cleaning. Best described as a vast pipeline of one-way valves and hundreds of filtering nodes, the lymphatic system helps our body remove waste and fight infection. Both movement and breathing are essential for lymphatic drainage. Breathing techniques can be used to optimise the process as well as protect us against harmful particles and microbes that would otherwise enter our lungs.

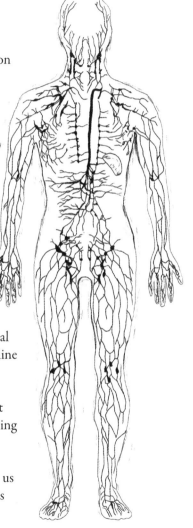

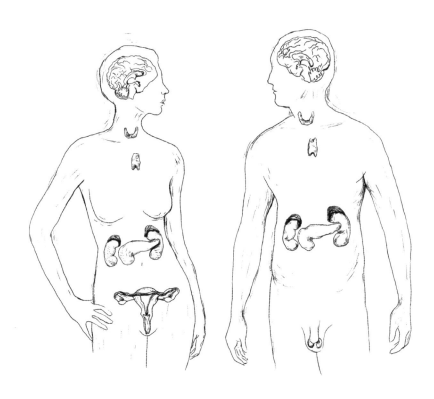

ENDOCRINE SYSTEM

Breath connects to hormones both directly and indirectly. For example, adrenaline directly changes breathing rate while thyroid hormones impact cell metabolism, indirectly changing respiration on a cellular level which can have a significant impact over the medium to long-term. By changing breathing, we can also alter how our body interprets the need for and processing of certain hormones. Breathing techniques can be used to support hormone balance, leading to improved energy levels and digestion as well as promoting restful sleep and optimising cell health.

COGNITIVE FUNCTION AND CONCIOUSNESS

How we think and interpret things impacts our breathing. Breathing techniques can improve focus, change thought patterns and can support or be used to accompany long term, meaningful change.

REPRODUCTIVE SYSTEM

Breath both impacts and is impacted by our reproductive system, organs, and associated hormones. Breathing techniques can enhance sexual function and aid hormonal balance.

INTEGUMENTRAY SYSTEM

Our skin, hair and nails mainly connect to breathing through the nervous and cardiovascular systems. Stimulation of nerves located in the skin can restrict breathing (such as exposure to cold and intense pain) or promote relaxed breathing through soothing touch (such as massage). Breathing techniques can help optimise body temperature, improve skin cell health, clear toxins and support change related to negative stimuli.

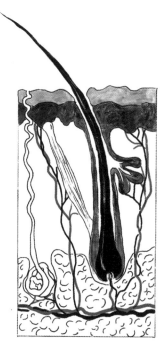

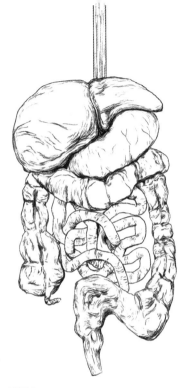

DIGESTIVE SYSTEM

The digestive and respiratory systems intertwine anatomically and through function. The oesophagus pierces through the middle of our main respiratory muscle, the diaphragm, and since this muscle rests on top of our stomach and intestines, the physical acts of breathing and digestion impact each other. The digestive system also makes up a large part of our enteric nervous system (ENS); often referred to as the "second brain," the ENS plays an active and important role in how we think and interpret the world around us. Breathing techniques can be used to soothe key elements of the digestive system, helping to create the optimum conditions for digestion as well as for our overall health and well-being.

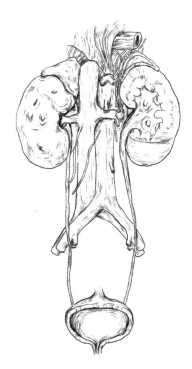

EXCRETORY SYSTEM

The excretory system mainly consists of the kidneys and bladder which help filter the blood of harmful waste products and assure internal homeostasis. One of the key parts of this balance is blood pH. Every cell within us, from muscles and neurons to organs and bones, require a pH which is slightly more alkaline than water (around 7.35). Both the respiratory and excretory systems work together to maintain this level. Failure to do so can be fatal. Breathing techniques can be used to optimise pH balance, taking pressure off the kidneys and supporting body-wide health and well-being.

Using Breathing Techniques Safely

Breathing techniques can be as strong and effective as any medication and as impactful as any psychological therapy or physical intervention.

Since we spend every living moment breathing, this statement may come as a shock, but as you practise breathing techniques, you will find it to become increasingly true. Something happens when we transition from breathing naturally, without awareness, to breathing consciously, with purpose. Breathing techniques are, in their most basic essence, safe for everyone but, considering their impact and interconnection with every part of us, they can also lead to trouble when used forcefully or disconnected from what we, as individuals, really need. For example: should you feel agitated or restless, engaging a technique that further stimulates you can trigger even deeper anxiety or emotional discomfort.

By maintaining a healthy regard for breathing techniques, we keep ourselves safe and open to their fuller potential. To assure yourself enjoyable practice, follow instructions carefully and remain aware of how you feel using each breath.

Important: None of the techniques in this book should cause harm or pain. If you feel discomfort during practice, stop for a moment; go for a walk, do some gentle exercise or rest. Usually, these are enough to restore balance. You can always try giving the breath another go later. Given our nature, nothing stays the same so returning to a breath a few weeks, or even months, later can make all the difference.

If you are pregnant or have undergone recent abdominal or thoracic surgery, avoid techniques with rapid changes in breath and posture and refrain from holding your breath for long periods. These guidelines are also suggested for people who have been diagnosed with:

- Aneurysm
- Chronic lung disorders
- Coronary Heart Disease
- Epilepsy
- Gastric Ulcer
- Hernia
- Mental health issues (including schizophrenia, mood disorders or any condition that leaves you feeling very anxious)
- Retina/eye issues

If you are unsure about any of the techniques or their effect on your health, please consult a local respiratory health practitioner for advice.

Are You Breathing Correctly?

———

To attain the most effective results from breathing techniques, it is helpful to know the breathing condition you are starting from. Depending on what you find, certain techniques will stand out as essential practice while others will prove particularly hard, at least in the beginning. Whatever you discover will prove invaluable! This chapter holds four simple tests that will help you identify your strengths and the potential challenges that may arise. You can record your results using the table on page 49.

Diaphragmatic vs. Chest Breathing

The diaphragm is the most efficient breathing muscle in the body but, since we do not need to use it, our body learns to use accessory muscles instead. Poor posture, excessive exercise and stress can lead to what is known as chest breathing. This happens when a collection of upper body muscles literally lift the chest to draw air in. This style of breathing is very energy-intensive since it uses muscles that are inefficient for the task of relaxed breathing. It also has the tendency to draw the belly inwards and upwards on inhalation. Since this pattern restricts our lungs from exchanging oxygen and carbon dioxide, we end up breathing faster than would otherwise be necessary.

WHY THIS IS IMPORTANT

If we think of ourselves as a car, engaging anything other than diaphragmatic breathing is like driving in a low gear; it puts excessive pressure on the heart and subjects our whole body to unnecessary stress and tension.

ESSENTIAL BREATHING TECHNIQUES

Practise *The Tap* (page 86) and *Diaphragmatic Breathing* (page 142) to help restore an optimum breathing pattern.

TEST 1

Lie down on the floor. Keep your knees bent
and shuffle to let your lower back relax.

Place one hand on your chest and the other
on your lower belly.

Observe which hand(s) you breathe into?

Diaphragmatic breathing (D) is recognisable when the
expansion takes place in the lower abdomen: inhalation
raises the lower belly and relaxes it on exhalation.

Chest breathing (C) is noted for exaggerated movement in
the chest. The upper chest rises during inhalation and falls
during exhalation.

Ensure to test your breathing in all body positions,
including seated and standing, as it varies.

TEST 2

While standing, place a weighted backpack evenly
on both shoulders.

Take a breath in; notice whether the backpack lifts upwards
(U) or remains (relatively) still (S) during breathing.

If you do not have a backpack, you can use your own palm,
one at a time (left palm on the right shoulder and vice versa).
Alternatively, it is interesting to practise with a friend; take it
in turns to place hands firmly on each other's
shoulders to create the weighted effect.

Breathing Rate

Interesting fact: At rest, the average person breathes four times more oxygen than they actually need. Even as you read this sentence, it is almost certain you are over-breathing!

WHY THIS IS IMPORTANT

It is an easy misconception that breathing more than we need might increase oxygen levels in our blood but, unfortunately, the opposite takes place. Over-breathing, as it is called, is counterproductive for how it expels excessive amounts of carbon dioxide. Through a chemical reaction known as the Bohr effect (see *Nil by Mouth* on page 90) clearing too much carbon dioxide makes it harder for cells to receive oxygen. An optimum balance of carbon dioxide is needed for ideal health and well-being.

ESSENTIAL BREATHING TECHNIQUES

Practise *Slow Motion* (page 108) and *4:7:8* (page 112) to help slow breathing rate to an optimum number of breaths per minute.

TEST 3

Set a timer for sixty seconds.

Count the number of breaths you take during this time.

Repeat three times to get an average.

What was your average number of breaths over a minute?

16+	STRONGLY OVER-BREATHING
9-15	OVER-BREATHING
4-8	SATISFACTORY
3	OPTIMUM
1	BREATHING MASTER

Breath-Holds

The length of time we can hold our breath during light exercise demonstrates a snapshot of our fitness; it shows our body's ability to distribute oxygen during physical exertion and our capacity to handle the rising levels of carbon dioxide resulting from the exercise itself.

WHY THIS IS IMPORTANT

Breath-holding demonstrates, very quickly, the health of our lungs, lung capacity and the efficiency of the body to distribute essential gases to the body. Interestingly, it also demonstrates our ability to handle both physiological and emotional stress to some degree.

ESSENTIAL BREATHING TECHNIQUES

Practise *Nil by Mouth* (page 90) and *The Dive* (page 152) to help develop fitness and breath-holding capabilities.

TEST 4

Using a stopwatch, breathe naturally for sixty seconds.

Once complete, inhale to fifty percent of your capacity, hold your breath and begin walking. Feel free to walk on the spot if you do not have space to move freely.

Stop the timer when you feel the first urge to breathe. Focus on when you need to breathe rather than how long you can hold our breath. This ensures you are testing breath-holding fitness rather than willpower.

How long did you last in seconds?

1-5	POOR FITNESS
6-19	BELOW SATISFACTORY
20-29	SATISFACTORY
30-54	OPTIMUM
55+	BREATHING ATHLETE

Do not be disheartened by what you discover. Remember: it is almost certain you have been breathing much more air than you have needed. This practical inevitability plays a huge role in giving low scores on this test. The good news is that improving this score is surprisingly easy.

The Importance of Retesting

Retest each of the four exercises every few weeks to help determine how you are progressing. If you do not notice any improvements within one month's practice, connect with a local breathworker or respiratory specialist to ensure you are completing the tests correctly and to help identify issues that may be getting in the way of your progress.

The table below can be used to record your results:

DATE:				
TEST 1	D / C	D / C	D / C	D / C
TEST 2	U / S	U / S	U / S	U / S
TEST 3	___ SECS	___ SECS	___ SECS	___ SECS
TEST 4	___ SECS	___ SECS	___ SECS	___ SECS

The Anti-Sit

——

Breathing techniques naturally restore and promote vitality but can lead us to experience the opposite of their intended effect. Discomfort, frustration and difficulty practising breathing techniques are par for the course! The reason for this is simple: twenty-first century living is hard on the body. Toxic environments, sedentary lifestyles and poor diets place unprecedented levels of stress and strain on us. It is almost certain everyone has, to some degree, strayed from their healthier breathing potential. *The Anti-Sit* is an antidote to twenty-first century living. Inspired by the essential breath and flow of yoga and Pilates, it instils natural, healthy movement back into the spine and can help us reclaim breathing capacity.

The Anti-Sit works by stimulating circulation, increasing lung capacity, and developing healthier, more uniform musculature. Practised regularly it improves our posture and brings balance to mind, body and spirit.

TIPS TO HELP

- Engage the muscles under your arms, middle back, and belly to offer extra buoyancy off the floor.
- Your elbows should be pointing backwards, like cricket legs, while in the rest position.
- Rather than holding your breath, breathe slowly and fully throughout the exercise.
- Ensure your eyes are open (rather than closed) during practice. Let your gaze be gentle.
- Take your time. It can take months, even a few years, to comfortably reach the full movement and dexterity this exercise demands. Most important of all, explore the pleasure and enjoyment of moving and breathing this way.

THE BREATH

Lying on your front, place palms flat on the floor in alignment with your armpits. Let your forehead rest on the floor.

Breathe into your back setting the intention to create space and length down the entire spine. Notice how each exhale can be used to relax your neck and upper back muscles.

Remaining in this position, practise lifting your belly muscles up off the floor while keeping your back muscles relaxed. Complete five belly lifts.

With belly muscles primed, next, use your arms and belly muscles to lift your whole upper torso forwards and upwards a few inches off the floor. Enjoy a few deep breaths in this lifted position. Feel how each inhalation creates space in your back and ribs.

Lie your body back down on its front. Let everything relax for a few breaths.

Repeat this sequence up to five times seeking to increase the upward lift until your arms are straight and both the front and back of your body feel long and stretched. To help, keep your head pressed backwards to create healthy muscle development of the upper and middle back.

Let everything relax for a few breaths before seating yourself backwards against your heels with arms stretched comfortably outwards.

Practise three times a day: morning, afternoon and before bed.

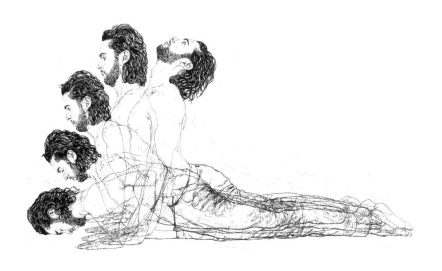

The 21 Breaths

———

One of my favourite conversations to have is how there is a breath for everything. I know most people think I'm joking but, actually, I really do mean it. There really *is* a breath for everything! Whether you need to fall asleep, require powerful pain relief or perhaps just want to supercharge your fitness and self-care routine; there are breathing techniques that will help you. So connected is your breath to your mind, body and spirit, that it can, quite simply, inspire the extraordinary. Here are the *21 Breaths* that will change your life.

1. BREATH TO RELIEVE PAIN
Mindful Breath

———

Mindful Breath is different from the usual breathing technique; consider it more of a breath observation than changing one's breath. Though hugely and positively impactful on pain, how it works is not as we might expect. At first, you will notice how the breath prepares the mind and body to experience pain differently.
At some point, and varying from person to person, perception itself changes. This breath is like a riddle: it is nothing before it becomes something and, when something begins, you will notice pain to, literally, evaporate into the thickness of a continually expanding awareness.

An immeasurable number of things happen around and within us. Since it is impossible to perceive everything that occurs, we become geared to pick up only a limited number of stimuli. These become repetitively hard-wired within us and lean towards either pleasure or discomfort. By concentrating solely on breathing sensations, these focal points are disturbed: pain-combatting tools are forged in the process, including focus and expanded awareness. Both of these tools enable attention to move from something painful towards something less overwhelming. In the process, our thoughts and experiences are challenged but, in time, we open up to something far deeper: the inevitability of change and how something like pain shifts, rather than stays constant. Also, by placing attention solely on our breath, we invite new, healthier patterns of breathing to emerge. In the beginning, *Mindful Breath* works by supporting us to feel less pain. With practice, reality itself is confronted and skills are developed that clear pain altogether.

TIPS TO HELP

- This breath takes time and patience. Let the breath remain natural and free rather than controlling it.

- Practise in a quiet, gently lit room first. In time you will be able to engage this breath anywhere.

- This technique is about sensation. It is surprisingly easy to switch from feeling the breath to hearing or internally visualising it. If you notice your awareness switch, gently return to feeling it instead.

- The aim of this breath is to maintain focus during slow, quiet breathing. In practice, this is can be challenging. To reclaim a wandering mind, breathe rapidly for ten seconds to help create stronger, more stimulating sensations. Use variances of breathing pace to help maintain focus whenever needed.

THE BREATH

Choose the best position for you. Shut your eyes and bring attention to the surface on the inside of your nostrils.

Inhale and exhale rapidly. Observe the sensation in and around your nose. Seek to reduce intensity over time towards ever quieter breathing.

Maintain focus by increasing and decreasing breathing intensity for ten minutes or as long as is needed.

Repeat every day (and more than once a day during periods of inflammation).

Develop length of observation by five minutes each week, up to sixty-minutes. Practise for longer should you wish.

2. BREATH FOR TIREDNESS

Celestial Lift

———

Contemporary lifestyles too easily throw our energy levels out of balance. We choose to be active when we could be resting and inactive when what we need is exercise. Conflict is the result, leaving us tired and feeling the need to make up the difference with stimulants and depressants. Over short periods of time, substances such as caffeine, sugar and medication can be highly effective but, used regularly, we are left feeling out of sorts, tormented by cravings, and harbouring that strange sensation of being both wired and exhausted at the same time.

Celestial Lift works with our breath's capacity to harness natural stimulation, offering a sustainable pick-me-up that only benefits long-term energy levels and metabolism. When we are tired, circulation is often sluggish and our body poorly oxygenated. *Celestial Lift* engages four key mechanisms to counter these symptoms: body shaking, spinal extension, breath-holding and lung ventilation. Body shaking helps to stimulate circulation and release tension; spinal extension also improves circulation but, more specifically, targets the nervous system, while breath-holding acts a multiplier effect for the other mechanisms and promotes cell oxygenation. Lastly, all of these combine to encourage dynamic changes in lung ventilation, improving our body's metabolic efficiency and ability to clear toxins. Perhaps the most interesting part of this technique is how it impacts heart rate and blood pressure. Through practice, you will actually be able to feel both lower considerably, particularly at the end of each cycle. Sensing the change, our body works to restore balance and, in the process, releases feel-good endorphins to leave us feeling refreshed and alert.

TIPS TO HELP

- It is possible to feel faint and even black out using this technique. On first practice, hold your breath for no more than five seconds and maintain awareness of your hands and feet. Increase breath-holding in small increments until clearer of its impact.

- This breath involves spinal extension. If this is uncomfortable for you, do some gentle stretching and exercise, such as *The Anti-Sit*, until discomfort lessens. Include some leg and hip stretches and use a foam roller to massage your spine.

- During spinal extension, let your shoulders, arms and spine remain relaxed.

THE BREATH

Standing, gently shake your body for three minutes. Take the time to notice specific areas of your body where you may be feeling tired or tense. If it feels OK, use the final sixty seconds to shake as vigorously as you can.

Wait for your body to return to natural breathing before moving on.

Find yourself a door frame or something secure
and upright to hold. Holding firmly, breathe in fully
through your nose and then hold your breath.

During the breath-hold, imagine a wave rising from your
feet up to the top of your head. Let your body extend
upwards towards the ceiling, as though mirroring this
sensation; both the front and back of your body should
feel long. You are in the perfect position if a strong stretch
develops along the top of your rib cage, collar bones and
throat. Ensure there is no tension in your back or neck.

Maintain this lifted breath-hold for a count of
five while keeping your feet grounded.

Exhale slowly and return to a neutral, standing position.

You may experience a strong feeling of lightheadedness.
Breathe naturally for a few minutes letting these sensations
subside before repeating up to another two cycles.

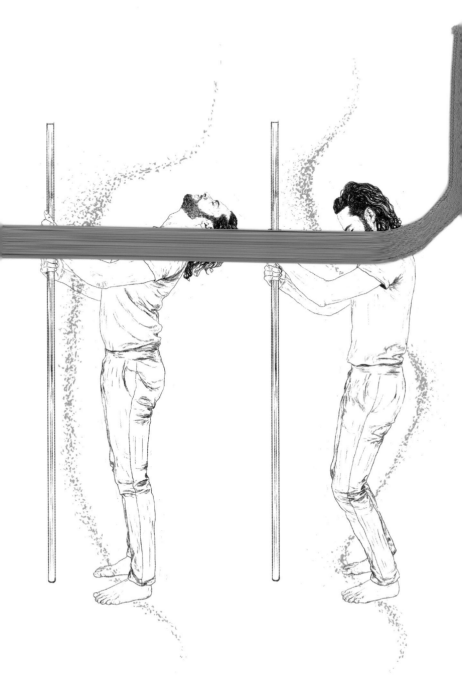

3. BREATH TO SLEEP

Rising Tide

———

A good night's rest offers unparalleled revitalisation of mind, body, and spirit and yet, despite its simplicity, hundreds of millions of us suffer sleep disorders every day. The greatest challenge we face is finding a remedy that is less impactful, in terms of side effects, than the disorder itself. The perfect solution would support restful sleep whenever we need it, be free from negative consequences and cost nothing to practise. Thank goodness for breath!

This breath works by deactivating the sympathetic nervous system and engaging key parts of the parasympathetic nervous system. It does this through carefully designed breathing movements, tension release and visualisation. What sets this technique apart from other sleep-supporting breaths is how it stimulates the yawn reflex. When engaged with the parasympathetic nervous system, the body is able to release sleep-inducing hormones and prepares itself for an amazing night's rest.

TIPS TO HELP

- Create a routine of switching off electronic screens, having a bath or doing some gentle stretching an hour before bedtime. These positive sleep hygiene steps are proven to encourage more restful sleep.

- Let your eyelids, face and whole body feel sleepy as you practise.

- Detach from the outcome of falling asleep. Though counterintuitive, this helps to free us from pressure which is unhelpful at bed

- Do not worry if this br appear to work during ment; developing a sense of an essential piece of the restful-night's-sleep puzzle and supercharges the effectiveness of this breath.

THE BREATH

Lying down on your back, shut your eyes and breathe deeply into your lower belly.

Holding your breath, squeeze every part of your body until you need to breathe.

Exhale. Notice how your exhale can be used to relax your body.

Let the next inhale be slower than the one before; filling from your lower body up to the collarbones, feel it stretch every part of your lower torso and each rib in turn.

As this wave-like sensation meets your collarbones, imagine the inhale to continue upwards. Placed correctly, your soft palate will feel to lift and broaden, like the sensation of a yawn.

Pause again at your inhale's peak. Once again, squeeze your entire body and then, as your exhale begins, let the whole body shed yet more tension.

Can you slow your breath down any further? Notice how each breath can be used to breathe into new areas of your body. Each time it reaches your collarbones, let it continue upwards, as before, lifting your soft palate and widening the back of your head.

Continue breathing this way for ten breaths.

Return to natural breathing for a few minutes. Repeat three cycles of ten breaths. Over-active mind? Complete the breath-hold and body squeeze after each cycle.

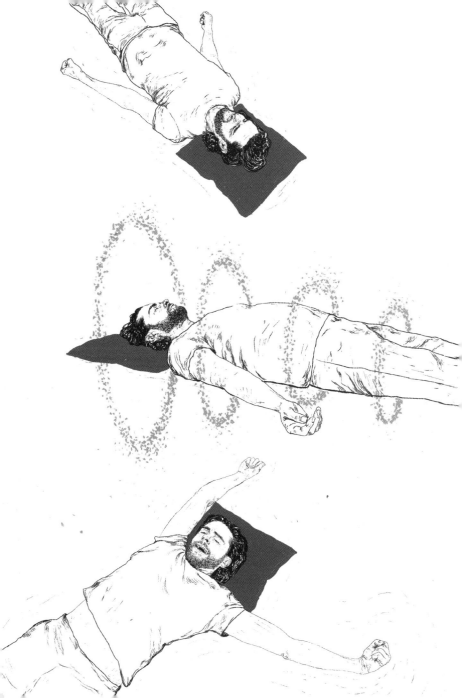

4. BREATH TO HELP YOU POOP

The Double Movement

———

The Double Movement is named for its remarkable ability to support two stool movements in one sitting. Did you even know you were capable of such a feat? Through practice everyone, including children, can learn to poop without strain, benefiting from breath's ability to ease constipation, bloating and trapped wind.

Firstly, this breath uses the exhale like a massage, gently soothing the abdominal area with its inner squeeze. Not only does this release tension and improve circulation; it also stimulates peristalsis, the natural wave-like contractions of the colon. Secondly, *The Double Movement* balances the nervous system; the fight-or-flight response is naturally deregulated while the rest-and-digest mechanisms are engaged. The combination of these mechanisms helps to access our enteric nervous system, also known as the "second brain." When in balance, the enteric nervous system is able to release messages to the entire body to combat the causes of stress, release tight muscles and encourage healthier bowel movements and cravings.

TIPS TO HELP

- The perfect time to practise this breath is when going to the toilet feels easy. Then we can experience how this breath is meant to feel and, subsequently, naturally install it into our body's memory.

- Spend time with the exhale; let it be slow and relaxed. You will notice the body engages a deeper contraction on its own, without requiring you to grip or push.

- Try lifting your heels off the floor, while keeping toes grounded, to help relax key muscles of the pelvis. Always let your arms relax should they get tired.

- If there is little progress with this breath, take a break. Wait until your body naturally readies for another movement. Taking the pressure off yourself is important, particularly during the first few occasions of practising this technique. It also helps to relieve tension and promote helpful muscle memory.

THE BREATH

Seated on the toilet, shut your eyes.

Breathe deep into your belly. Relax as you exhale.

At the top of the next inhale, hold your breath for a moment before sipping more air in. At first, this ballooning sensation can feel intense but notice that you can relax into it.

When it is time to exhale, do so slowly. Feel how, as you exhale, your whole core starts to hug you like a broad belt: the front, sides and even around the back. Remember these sensations as you will need them while practising this breath.

RIGHT

Reach both arms towards the ceiling with interlocked fingers. Side bend over to the left allowing a stretch down your right side. Practise the sip-inhalations in this position. Fill your entire right side, like a balloon. Let your head rotate towards your right elbow (while it rests on your left arm) to relax the belly more.

Maintaining this stretch, exhale, seeking that smooth and even lower-body hug. Continue breathing this way, balloon inhaling and hug exhaling for two to three breathing cycles. Return to neutral and repeat this sequence on the other side.

Returning to neutral, re-interlock your fingers and, this time, reach upwards and backwards if you can. You may even be able to rest your head and arms against the back wall. Practise sipping air deep into your lower ribcage before exhaling and returning to a neutral seated position.

BELOW

Finally, take a breath in and fold forwards. Let your torso rest on your knees as you sip-inhale into your lower back and pelvis. Let the exhale return you back to a neutral position. Repeat this around the world cycle another two times, taking time to rest in between.

5. BREATH TO CLEAR A COLD

Nose Unblocking Exercise

———

There is nothing like a blocked nose and aching sinuses to remind us of just how impactful impaired breathing can be. Not only do we contend with a heavy head but it makes for restless sleep and can leave us feeling groggy and irritable the following day. Medication and decongestants are useful but, some of the ingredients actually damage the sensitive skin in our nose and even used a few times can be habit forming. What we need is a remedy we can use anytime, anywhere, to clear our head. For effectiveness, Patrick McKeown's *Nose Unblocking Exercise* is one of the most powerful and natural decongestants.

McKeown speaks of how mouth breathing causes blood vessels in the nose to become inflamed and how, when we have a cold, this mechanism becomes exacerbated and further contributes to the negative cycle. By engaging this technique, we encourage the release of a neurotransmitter called nitric oxide. This helps to improve circulation around the nose and sinuses, freeing airways and returning us to healthier nose breathing. Nitric oxide improves circulation and oxygenation, enabling our breathing rate to slow and ensuring optimum levels of oxygen and carbon dioxide for health and well-being. Importantly, I feel how this breath gently stimulates the sympathetic nervous system (the fight-or-flight mechanism), which naturally triggers internal messages that automatically unblock airways.

TIPS TO HELP

- You will be pinching your nose and holding your breath for this exercise. Relax and observe sensations arising from this action; connecting with a sense of inner enquiry makes for a fascinating and almost enjoyable experience.
- Drink half a glass of water a few minutes before engaging.

THE BREATH

Standing upright, take a small, silent breath in and a silent breath out (through your nose if able!)

Keeping the breath out, pinch your nose with your fingers and hold your breath.

Walk as many paces as possible while keeping the nose pinched. Aim to build up a strong air shortage without overdoing it.

When you resume breathing, aim to do so through your nose only.

If your breath feels strained, work to suppress your second and third breaths rather than gasping through your mouth.

If you still feel breathless after a couple of breaths, you have held your breath for too long. Experiment releasing the nose-pinch earlier next time.

Wait for one minute before resuming the next round.

Repeat five or six cycles of this breath or until your nose clears.

(Adapted with permission from *The Oxygen Advantage*, 2015)

6. BREATH FOR MIND-BLOWING SEX

The Ripple

————

Have you noticed how breathing changes dramatically during sex? We can use this respiratory connection to turn breath into orgasm gold. Breathing techniques have been used for thousands of years to enhance sexual pleasure; though highly effective, many well-known methods do not always feel practical within an intimate connection. *The Ripple* is different; it is a technique that anyone can use. Engaging breath, movement and focus, it is possible to breathe ourselves towards a deeper sensual experience that only builds with practise.

Research has proven that sexual experiences can be enhanced by combining conscious awareness with a flowing, relaxed breath. By learning to develop whole-body pleasure (rather than solely focusing on our erogenous zones), both our potential for sexual longevity and euphoria are enhanced with pleasurable, wave-like contractions activated throughout the body.

TIPS TO HELP

- It helps to practise by oneself first, before using with a partner.

- Before and during orgasm, bring attention to the middle of your forehead. This helps teach us the skills we need to experience deeper, whole-body sensations.

- Experiment letting go of thoughts and judgements. Should they arise, deepen your breath and sensual movement. It is when we release ourselves from our usual tension and restraint that this breath excels.

- Choosing to retain the charge this breath creates, rather than orgasming, is powerful. Should you choose not to climax, ensure to send all of the built-up charge evenly around your body with your hands and imagination. Your groin may ache for a time, but this sensation will subside and leave you feeling very energised.

- Ensure you have warm hands!

THE BREATH

Lying down, hold your genitals with one hand and place the other hand on your lower belly. Gently squeeze and release to bring focus these parts of your body.

Shut your eyes and breathe deeply towards the warmth created by both hands. Some people notice colours as they breathe here. Enjoy their pattern and intensity if they do.

After a few minutes of gentle, pelvic breathing, deepen your breath. Allow it to be slow and sensual. Notice how it encourages your lower back to arch softly during inhalation and curl forwards during exhalation.

Maintained, this stimulating breath and movement creates a tingling sensation that strengthens over time. It can feel an emotional, almost confusing experience; waves of joy interspersed with tension and frustration. Keep going. Continue breathing. Continue rocking. And continue letting go.

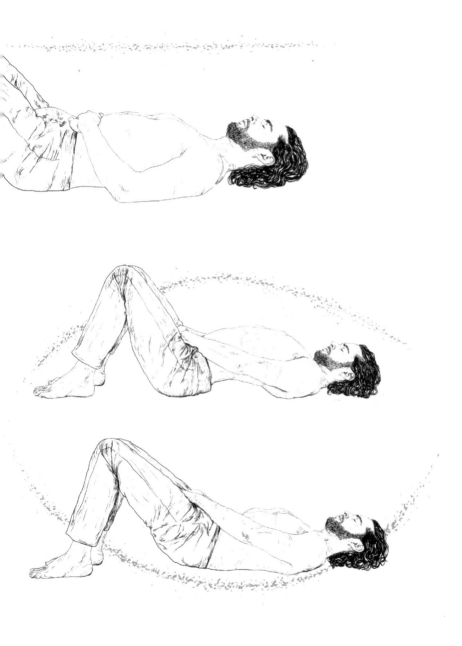

Once the charge feels palpable, experiment moving this charge (and colours!) around your body with your palms and your imagination. Follow your impulse. There is no right or wrong; anything that feels pleasurable and sensual is welcome. If it feels new or you feel unsure, try swapping your palms, one exchanged for the other. A sweeping sensation, from groin to belly and back again, helps tap into our more primal instincts.

Once built, let this charge run up your spine. Watch it run down your legs. Send it to your fingertips. Let yourself be coloured in by the charge and tingling. Lovemaking may now begin!

There is no need to orgasm to benefit from this technique but, should climax build, rather than focusing on your genitals (which is easy to do), instead bring attention to the centre of your forehead; to access your orgasm potential, imagine allowing the charge to flow like waves from here to every part of your body.

7. BREATH TO LOWER BLOOD PRESSURE

The Tap

___

Worryingly, blood pressure appears to be on the rise. In western cultures alone, close to half of the adult population are impacted; ageing and genetics are cited as contributors but stressful lifestyles, smoking, poor diet and lack of exercise also play a large role. Though medication is effective, the underlying cause of high blood pressure is rarely improved. Blood pressure medications can have complicated side effects, too, including dehydration and reduction in heart function. Breathing techniques offer an effective, low cost and natural solution with minimal side effects and a host of other health benefits.

Making use of nasal diaphragmatic breathing promotes whole-body efficiency, consumes less energy than mouth breathing and releases neurotransmitters that help dilate blood vessels. Slowing the breath and breathing through the nose also raises carbon dioxide levels. Paradoxically, this improves circulation and cellular oxygenation and further relaxes blood vessels. Lastly, this technique calms an active mind: by stabilising emotions and relieving stress, the body learns to recuperate more effectively while the heart works less for greater output.

TIPS TO HELP

- Your breath will naturally lengthen over time using this technique. Feel free to stretch the count should it feel good to do so.

- Let your breathing remain gentle throughout practice. Exaggerating or applying force only counters its effect.

- Play some relaxing music or recall how it felt to be on a relaxing holiday. Remembering restful, feel-good experiences enhances the effect of this technique.

- You will be engaging tension-release exercises during this breath. Over time, your body will learn to let go without needing to physically squeeze itself beforehand. Practising this skill will help you to engage the technique at times when you may otherwise feel uncomfortable doing so, like at work or out in public.

THE BREATH

Sit yourself in a comfortable position. Shut your eyes.

Take a deep inhale through your nose allowing the air to travel downwards, towards your belly. Pause a moment before exhaling. Take a moment to appreciate your body.

On your next inhale, breathe in for a count of five. Notice that a softness is required to allow your breath to travel downwards. Pause a moment before exhaling.

At the top of your next five-count inhale, hold your breath a little longer. During this pause, squeeze every muscle, from head to toe.

Exhale when you need to. Let the exhale support you to release any tension you may be holding.

Inhale for a count of five; pause; squeeze all your muscles and, again, let everything go on the exhale.

Repeat this inhale-hold-contract-exhale-surrender cycle for ten minutes.

Practise twice daily. Consider developing towards two twenty-minute sessions after one month's practice to maintain and enhance effects.

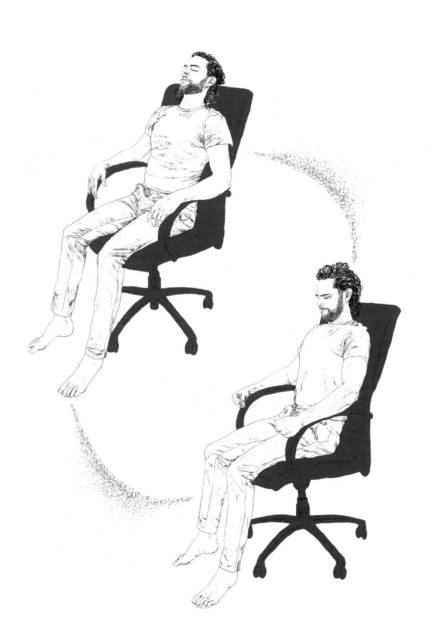

8. BREATH TO IMPROVE FITNESS

Nil by Mouth

———

Fitness seen through the eyes of breathing introduces a paradox: breathing less helps us to respire more! At first glance, this may not make sense, so let's break it down. As we increase physical intensity our body demands that we breathe more. Should we limit our breathing while our body demands more air, fitness grows because our body develops the ability to exchange and deliver essential gases and nutrients more efficiently. Unfortunately, the process does not work in reverse. Should we breathe more than our body requires (for example, through hyperventilation) the whole process turns upside down and we, literally, lose fitness.

Exercise has a unique impact on respiration; as intensity increases, breathing increases also. The reason for this surge is not as we might expect: rather than fulfilling oxygen needs, the body is programmed to clear carbon dioxide. The brain stem is responsible for this process and works to keep carbon dioxide concentration within optimum parameters.

The brain stem operates, in part, from a place of history. How we have breathed in the past and what feels normal plays a huge role in this respect. Two people can have different concentrations of carbon dioxide in their blood and yet feel the same... regardless of oxygen levels!

Nil by Mouth dramatically improves fitness for four reasons. Firstly, the breath harnesses our body's natural respiratory inhibitor, the nose, to increase carbon dioxide levels in our blood. In turn, the body increases carbon dioxide resilience. This allows us to handle higher levels of this gas without requiring deeper breathing or a faster heart rate. Secondly, cells in our body receive more oxygen when carbon dioxide levels increase. This happens through a process known as the Bohr effect, a chemical reaction that causes red blood cells to drop the oxygen atoms they carry. This creates a win-win situation for muscles as it supports their metabolic requirement for oxygen, particularly important during exercise when demand for oxygen is far greater. Thirdly, nasal breathing releases a gas called nitric oxide. This acts as a neurotransmitter, helping to dilate blood vessels and improve both lung function and circulation. Ultimately, this takes pressure off the heart. Lastly, extra red blood cells are created when we are subject to prolonged periods of air hunger. Like breathing at altitude, our respiratory efficiency naturally improves under these conditions.

TIPS TO HELP

- This is a simple breath but the experience of it can be overwhelming. Start slowly; it is recommended you exercise at sixty percent of your usual capacity and build from there.

- Slow down or do less rather than revert to mouth breathing. It is when this technique feels tough that its true potential is unlocked! Ensure you remain relaxed during practice.

THE BREATH

The best time to begin this breath is ten minutes before you start your chosen exercise.

While exercising, breathe in through your nose. Breathe out through your nose. Repeat.

Keep breathing this way no matter your physical exertion.

Continue nasal breathing for at least a few hours after exercise and permanently for best results.

9. BREATH TO FEEL CONFIDENT

Bull Breath

How we feel intimately connects with breath; from the flowing breath of happiness to the tight, staccato-like gasps that choke to the surface when we hold in feelings of sadness. Confidence has feelings and sensations of its own; take the time to observe your breath during moments when you feel safe and secure. What breathing patterns and characteristics are present? *Bull Breath* utilises our emotion's connection to breath and posture to instil a positive and lasting feeling of confidence.

It is interesting to reflect on how a group of people can experience the same situation differently. This is, in part, due to how we experience emotions, which may best be described as chemical messengers of potential. From the latest research, it appears the brain and other key organs release these messengers all the time, however it takes coming into contact with specific parts of our body for them to be felt. We don't always notice this happening but, when we do, feelings arise. As you can imagine, feelings are complex. Not only do we each have varying ideas of what is positive or negative, we also relate to our past experience differently.

The process of decoding these chemical messengers is usually unconscious. However, by making it conscious we can, to some degree, choose how we feel. *Bull Breath* works through the interconnection of breath, posture and intention, allowing us to layer more consciously derived messengers over the top of any unconfident feelings we might be experiencing. By engaging this method in earnest, it is possible to instigate an immediate shift in our experience and, by changing our feelings, instil a sense of empowerment and confidence instead.

TIPS TO HELP

- Complete this breath standing to encourage a sense of groundedness and strength.
- Posturing is important. Every muscle in your body should feel engaged. Explore exhaling using your deepest abdominals.
- Bring the lower jaw forward so both sets of teeth are together, or, place the lower set just in front of the upper; as though sticking your jaw out.
- Avoid putting pressure on your teeth. Explore engaging your jaw muscles only.
- Engaging this technique with someone you trust can dramatically boost *Bull Breath's* effect. Eye contact is powerful. Try asking a friend or work colleague to join you and allow the breath to feel meaningful.
- Go wild with this breath!

THE BREATH

Standing, start by feeling your weight evenly balanced on your feet. Rise up onto your toes and, engaging mini jumps, let your heels strike the floor. Intensify hopping towards full jumps if you are able.

After twenty hops, return to standing. Keeping your knees slightly bent, tense all the muscles of your leg and buttocks to create a sense of solidity and groundedness.

Raising your arms up ninety degrees, with elbows and fists held tight (imagine a strongman pose), press your shoulders backwards and downwards. Allow your upper and lower body to feel strong.

Make a face like an angry bull. Breathe strongly and rapidly through both nose and mouth. Bring a challenging thought (or even a person!) to mind and let your facial expression and breath intensify.

Breathe this way, powerfully, for thirty seconds. Repeat three times, or as many times as helps you to feel empowered.

10. BREATH TO HELP PUBLIC SPEAKING

The Hum

———

Most of us enjoy speaking with family and friends, but few of us relish the opportunity to do so, formally, in front of a group or in public. We can learn a lot from the professionals: they take their time, find pleasure in the process and, most interestingly of all, breathe with grace and ease. By relieving our body's fear response and connecting to our inner flow, it's possible to harness the same emotional-physiological mechanisms as experienced public speakers.

A little stress can be helpful for focus and engagement when speaking in public but, should it be over-stimulating, it can tip us over an edge in a way that tightens our body in all the wrong places. One of the main culprits for this tension-creating impact is the sympathetic nervous system. Neurotransmitters and hormones released by this system restrict breathing muscles and tighten soft tissue all around our voice box, throat and abdomen.

The Hum works by transitioning us from chest-led hyper-ventilation towards slower, deeper diaphragmatic breathing. It also helps to redirect our attention from what may have been causing us stress towards something practical and calming. The superpower of this technique resides in its use of vibration. The natural resonance of our voice literally vibrates nerve endings which can calm the body. When combined with relaxed breathing, it is possible to activate our parasympathetic nervous system. Related to the process of rest and digestion, this system helps to counter stress-induced hormones by releasing its own calming hormones and neurotransmitters. Humming also releases nitric oxide, which helps support the function of the cardiovascular system to further take pressure off our body. Lastly, humming harnesses the resonance of our skull and airspaces within the upper respiratory tract to improve vocal resonance and tone.

TIPS TO HELP

- When under pressure, be mindful of your body's natural inclination to grip or force.
- Focus on a full but slow inhale and relaxed exhale.
- Be gentle if your voice feels tired or weak.
- Move the jaw from side to side to relax the muscles of the voice, neck, and lower abdomen.

THE BREATH

Standing upright, place both hands on your lower belly. Take a breath in. Where does your inhale travel?

Explore relaxing and deepening your breath as though breathing into your palms. Notice how each inhale stretches the lower abdomen and how every exhale relaxes it.

Breathe ten deep, relaxed breaths this way.

Over the next set of ten breaths, begin to hum; explore stretching the humming sound without tension being allowed to set in.

Shut your eyes. What sensations can you feel from humming?

OVERLEAF

Play with the power and effortlessness of your hum while moving in all directions.

Breathe and hum this way for ten minutes exploring where feels good and pleasurable for you.

Return palms to belly and breathe, as you did at the start, for a final three minutes.

11. BREATH FOR NAUSEA

Magical 2:1

———

There are many reasons a body can feel nauseous, from strong emotions and disruptive travel to intense movement and diet. It is important to remember that the process of vomiting can be necessary when harmful contents need to be expelled. Should we wish to clear feelings of nausea, we need an intelligent technique: one that can relieve discomfort without getting in the way of life-saving mechanisms.

The body responds with relatively defined breathing patterns when experiencing nausea: the diaphragm and abdominal muscles tighten, breath shortens, and we usually switch from nose to mouth breathing. Lengthening the exhale can help calm our body but, from the perspective of nausea, can worsen how we feel because the same muscles we use for breathing out also help expel contents from our stomach. *Magical 2:1* lengthens the inhale to exhale ratio, helping to avoid these muscles altogether and offering them a counter stretch instead.

When slow, expansive breathing is combined with a sense of sleepiness, it is possible to engage the parasympathetic nervous system, releasing soothing neurotransmitters and hormones that calm nausea and balance internal acid production.

TIPS TO HELP

- Ensure you are in a quiet, safe place.
- The optimum posture for this breath is seated in a relaxed, reclined position. The front of your hips and belly should feel soft and open.
- During each inhalation, take the time to notice how breathing stretches and relaxes your abdomen and ribs. These areas have a never-ending capacity to release tension.
- Think sleepy! Let the muscles around your eyes and jaw soften, as they might when we feel tired. Let this softening sensation ripple throughout your body.
- If you feel hot, imagine clearing heat from your body using an open mouth exhale, like fogging up a mirror.
- Focus on how gentle your breathing can be.

THE BREATH

Seated in a relaxed position, shut your eyes and take a slow, full breath in through your nose.

Hold your breath for a moment before letting the warm air in your lungs pour out through your mouth. There is no need to push the air out, let your body's natural elasticity do the work for you.

On your next inhale, see if you can let your breath stretch further into your lower abdomen. Allow a gentle pause at the top of the inhale, before letting your exhale go.

Continue this effortless, heat-clearing breath for ten minutes or until nausea subsides. It is a great sign if you to notice the muscles and skin around your lower belly and ribs begin to twitch.

Aim to be slow and mindful for an hour or so afterwards.

Repeat as necessary.

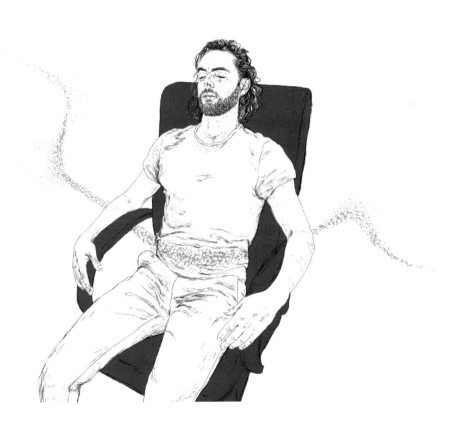

12. BREATH TO RELIEVE ASTHMA

Slow Motion

———

It is concerning that the number of people diagnosed with asthma appears to be on the rise. Not only is asthma a debilitating and potentially life-threatening condition but what causes it is not well understood. While there are medications to help relieve symptoms, to date, none offer a cure. *Slow Motion* targets the means through which our body can exacerbate the condition. It offers a chance to develop a positive, natural solution, that both helps during an attack and alleviates asthma's impact over time.

The throat and bronchial tubes are lined with sensitive tissue and nerves that act like a computer processor. They analyse the contents of our airways and function to keep us free from harmful bodies and particles. For someone experiencing asthma, the processor is hypersensitive. *Slow Motion* engages key elements to help reduce this sensitivity: nasal breathing, resistance, and respiratory efficiency.

Compared to mouth breathing, nose breathing is vastly more effective at filtering, humidifying and optimising lung air temperature. It also increases levels of nitric oxide which improves both cardiovascular and respiratory efficiency and our body's ability to fight pathogens. The resistance element of this breath trains our breathing muscles to operate differently. The result is easier, more relaxed breathing that is proven to be less reactive and inflamed over time. From an efficiency perspective, this breath also develops our carbon dioxide resilience which improves fitness and helps oxygenate our body.

TIPS TO HELP

- Where possible, use nose breathing to complete this breath.
- Practise inhaling slower with each breath until it is possible to barely feel the sensation of breathing at all.
- You will be using your arms to create respiratory resistance. During practice, imagine giving yourself a big hug rather than engaging with the tension aggressively.

THE BREATH

Find a comfortable position standing or seated.
Wrap both arms around the lower ribs so that
your hands gently hug your upper waist.

Shut your eyes. Take a slow breath in through your
nose, deep into your lower belly. Notice how your
arms offer a gentle resistance; breathe downwards,
past your arms, towards the lower belly.

During each exhale, notice how relaxed your body can get.
In particular, soften your face, throat, neck and chest.

On your next inhale, once it has dropped downwards
towards the belly, let it begin to fill you, like a jug,
from the bottom upwards.

Take time to notice how your lungs and torso
feel as they stretch during each inhale and how
your whole body can relax on the exhale.

Imagine how it would be to allow every
breath to deepen and slow.

Develop this breath by pausing, both at the peak of
the inhale and base of the exhale. Pause for as long
as you can without gripping or causing stress.

Repeat ten times.

13. BREATH TO RELEASE ANXIETY

4:7:8

———

This is one of the most famous breathing techniques in the world. It seems like everyone loves this breath, from researchers and doctors to yoga practitioners and breathworkers alike. Based on yogic pranayama principles, *4:7:8* has proven itself to not only effectively calm anxiety, but also lower heart rate and improve digestion. Thousands of articles have been written about this technique for its ability to relieve anxiety and promote deep relaxation.

The symptoms of anxiety, including hyperventilation, an elevated heart rate and intense feelings of nervousness and being overwhelmed, are all positively impacted by distinct elements of this breath. Firstly, the ratio of inhale to exhale is helpful; holding one's breath and then slowly letting it out changes carbon dioxide levels. This molecule plays an essential role in body chemistry: fast, anxious respiration clears carbon dioxide too rapidly which excites neuron activity and leads to restlessness.

Increasing carbon dioxide levels does the opposite: neuron activity is calmed, and restlessness subsides.

Secondly, this breath requires focus and concentration which further helps to calm an overstimulated mind. Combined with a slower breathing rate, *4:7:8* quietens the fight-or-flight reflex that plagues anxiety while tapping into the restorative capabilities of the parasympathetic system. With regular practice, the results can be long-lasting.

TIPS TO HELP

- The numbers that inspire the name of this breath are best viewed as a ratio rather than a duration of time in seconds. Feel free to stretch the duration of each part: inhalation, breath-hold and exhalation, respecting the ratio between each of them.
- Do not worry if this breath does not appear to work the first few times of using it. Its impact increases with practice.
- Practise maintaining as little tension as you can by relaxing your face, neck and body during each exhale.

THE BREATH

Lying down or seated, complete a full inhale and exhale to refresh the air in your lungs.

Shutting your eyes, place your tongue at the ridge of tissue behind the top front teeth. Maintain this position for the duration of the breath.

Breathe in through your nose for a count of four.

Hold the breath in for a count of seven.

Breathe out through your mouth for a count of eight. The exhale should be firm enough to make a whooshing sound, yet measured to last the count.

Reclose your mouth and repeat the *4:7:8* cycle.

Complete four *4:7:8* cycles before resting.

Relax in between rounds but feel free to practice the entirety of this breath another three times, or as necessary.

14. BREATH FOR THE NERVOUS FLYER

Geometric Breathing™

Despite being documented as the safest mode of travel, it is understandable how many people feel anxious about flying; it requires us to surrender ourselves into the hands of another, 5000 metres up in the air! Despite circumstances seeming out of control we can, at least, look after our breathing. *Geometric Breathing*™ is a game that uses geometric patterns and breath to invoke emotional and physical balance.

Our body's stress response is intricately linked to breath through pace, volume, and pattern. *Geometric Breathing*™ offers a fun way to experiment with this relationship and demonstrates, through practical experience, how we can harness mind and body through breath to move us from one psychophysiological state to another. *Geometric Breathing*™ also highlights our unique strengths and weaknesses while opening an internal dialogue about how breath can be used for calm and focus during moments that feel out of our control.

TIPS TO HELP

- These breaths are not suitable during pregnancy.
- Always begin each game with a full but gentle inhalation and exhalation.
- Unless you are directed to wear your seatbelt, you can choose to be either standing or seated.
- *Geometric Breathing*™ patterns develop in challenge and intensity. Ensure to stay within the edges of your comfort zone. This helps ensure progress over time.
- You are welcome to "count" in your head but, otherwise, use a clock or stopwatch to accurately track progress.

THE BREATHS

Starting at the centre, inhale for two seconds.
Exhale for two seconds.

Inhale for three seconds. Exhale for three seconds.

Continue to increase inhalation and exhalation by one
second until reaching a comfortable maximum.

Once you have reached your comfortable maximum,
shut your eyes and maintain its pattern for five minutes.

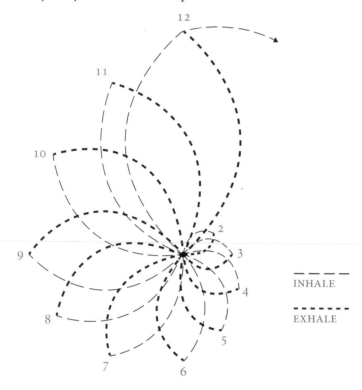

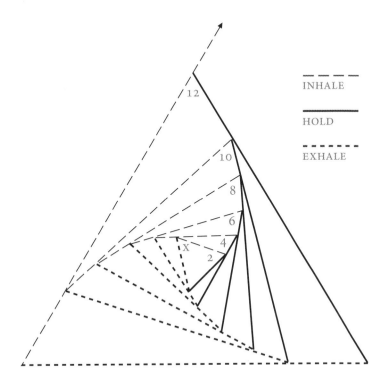

INHALE

HOLD

EXHALE

Starting at X, inhale for two seconds. Hold your breath for two seconds. Exhale for two seconds.

Inhale for three seconds. Hold your breath for three seconds. Exhale for three seconds.

Continue increasing each part of the breathing triad by one second until reaching a comfortable maximum.

Once you have reached your comfortable maximum, shut your eyes and maintain its pattern for five minutes.

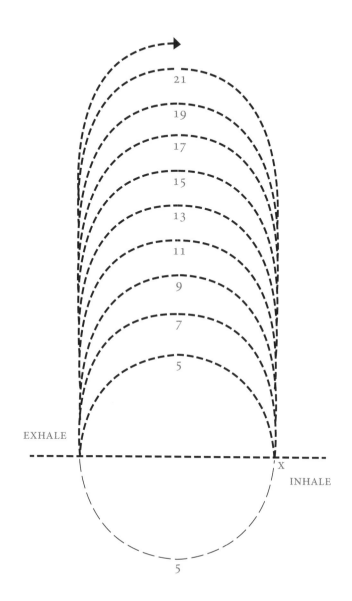

21

19

17

15

13

11

9

7

5

EXHALE

X

INHALE

5

Starting at X, inhale for a count of five seconds.
Exhale for five seconds.

Inhale for five seconds. Exhale for 7 seconds.

Continuing to inhale for five seconds while stretching
exhalation by two seconds more on each round
until reaching a comfortable maximum.

Once you have reached your comfortable maximum,
shut your eyes and maintain its pattern for five minutes.

15. BREATH TO HEAL A RELATIONSHIP

The Affirmation

——

We are surrounded by relationships. Obvious ones include family and friends, but subtler relationships also exist, including our relationship with ourselves and things such as food and possessions. Since breath and how we feel strongly intertwine, the two hold up a fascinating mirror to each other and show how breath, itself, can be a means to support positive emotional change.

The Affirmation works on multiple levels: firstly, it is important to remember that what we think and feel are perceptions. Since each of us think and feel differently, it is possible to create positive experiences from challenging ones. By using breath to impact our nervous system and positive imagery to change our feelings, we can fundamentally alter interpretation and long-held, negative narrative.

Perhaps the most important feature of *The Affirmation* is that it does not require the trigger to be present. By working on ourselves, this breath naturally enables everyone involved to experience its effect also. *The Affirmation* engages tools that positively impact our whole body: when we feel differently, the other party does too.

TIPS TO HELP

- Relationships can be chosen from the past, present, or future.
- This breath uses affirmations to embody a feeling or intention. This will be completed in the form of "I am." For example: "I am loving. I am forgiving."
- If you feel uncertain, start with an affirmation of safety such as "I am safe." With practice, you will be able to affirm any feeling or intention.
- If what arises relates to yourself, consider amending "I am" to "you are." Connecting through the second person can help the subconscious receive *The Affirmation* more easily.
- This breath taps into the wisdom of the heart, as opposed to the wisdom of the mind. How the heart expresses itself can seem strange at first: images, colours and feelings rather than words or clear sentences. Relax and enjoy the process if this feels new.

THE BREATH

Standing or seated, place your hands together in a prayer position and shut your eyes. Bring attention to the centre of your heart. Use an inhale to inspire an orb of light to form here.

Watch as every breath grows this orb in radiance and warmth.

Staying connected to this light, bring attention to the space between your palms. Let the relationship you wish to heal form its own orb, here. Spend a moment noticing how both orbs differ in colour and feeling.

Returning to your heart's light, pose the question: "What may heal this relationship?" Allow time for your heart to express itself. What do you notice and how does it feel?

At the top of your next inhale, infuse these feelings with the words "I am." To do this, state the words "I am", and then let your heart fill in the space afterwards.

Watch as this presence radiates outwards, surrounding you and the orb in your palms.

Repeat another six breaths allowing the essence of what comes up to deepen. Explore how it feels to guide your heart's healing energy into your palms and how it embraces the challenging relationship.

To finish, bow gently as a sign of gratitude for everything you might have learnt and gained in your life from this challenging relationship.

Watch your heart's light dissolve inwards. Relax your arms and return to natural breathing.

16. BREATH TO RELIEVE STRESS

The Cleanse

———

How we perceive stress can play an important role in determining the impact it has on our emotional and physical well-being. Many people assume stress to be negative, but it can also have positive outcomes. *The Cleanse* works to reduce the negative impact while harnessing our capacity for stimulation and growth under pressure.

The human body is an incredibly effective stress-responding machine. This is, in part, due to how our nervous system works. When we experience a threat to life, it is the sympathetic nervous system that engages; key neurotransmitters and hormones are released that prime us for action. Should we need to jump out of the way of an oncoming bus or escape a dangerous predator, these qualities are essential but since a similar reaction takes place when responding to work deadlines or during an argument with loved ones, it is typically excessive and detrimental.

The Cleanse engages strong, whole-body contractions with breath-holds and tension release to use up the stress-induced neurotransmitters. It also engages layers of relaxation, sighing and natural breathing in order to stimulate the rest-inducing parasympathetic nervous system, helping to return us to balance. Since the sympathetic and parasympathetic nervous systems function independently, it is possible for them to run side by side, before one takes the lead over the other.

TIPS TO HELP

- Avoid straining yourself while applying progressive muscle relaxation.
- Try tensing different parts of the body before whole-body engagement.
- If your face turns red during practice, you may be pushing too hard. Engage this technique compassionately.

THE BREATH

This technique can be completed using either nose or mouth breathing and in any position of your choice: standing, seated or lying down.

Take a few minutes to scan yourself for stress and tension. It can be sensed differently depending on its location in our body, thoughts or emotions.

Breathe in strongly and fully.

Holding your breath, gently squeeze every muscle in your body for five counts.

When you come to exhale, let the air whoosh out of your lungs with an audible sigh.

Repeat four more cycles, increasing the breath-hold and muscular engagement with each cycle.

After the last contraction, gently shake your entire body to release any remaining tension.

Take some time to reconnect. How do you feel?

Repeat another two times or as often as necessary.

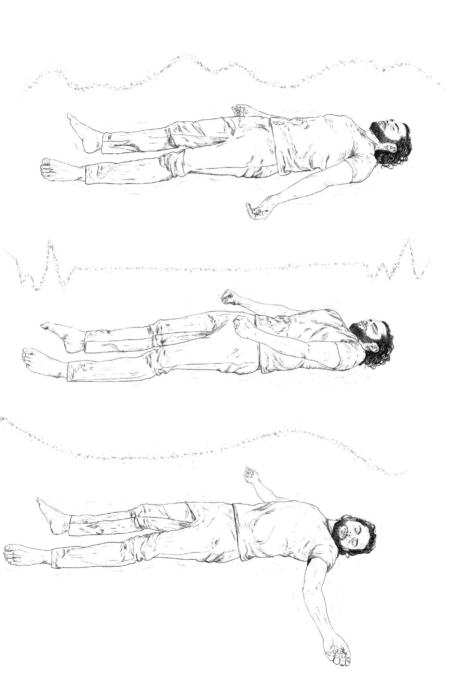

17. ANTI-AGEING BREATH

Waterfall

———

Did you know breathing contributes to ageing? The problem lies in how our cells use oxygen: by metabolising energy and oxygen, toxic by-products are created including carbon dioxide and free radicals. One of the keys to anti-ageing is ensuring efficient clearance of these harmful toxins; alongside a balanced diet of whole foods, vitamins and minerals, research shows breathing in specific ways helps to slow the ageing process.

Our body is using energy all the time. Often, incredibly inefficiently. This technique harnesses movement and breath to reduce some of its most energy-depleting responses to stress, including heightened respiratory and cardiovascular output. Our whole body benefits because, rather than focusing on completing wasteful, energy-intensive activities, energy is freed up for other health-promoting functions. Since metabolising is an oxidative process, any technique that improves efficiency and reduces waste will help slow ageing over time. In addition, diaphragmatic breathing helps to bring balance to the autonomic nervous system, further supercharging our body's function and efficiency. Breathing through the nose captures maximum levels of a neurotransmitter called nitric oxide; labelled the "mighty molecule" in 2011, NO continues to prove its anti-ageing properties by improving circulation, minimising cardiovascular effort and maintaining telomere integrity (the health of the end sections of our chromosomes that shorten as we age). The jumping and roll down elements help shed tension, improve posture, boost circulation, and encourage toxin clearance through lymphatic drainage. This technique is a veritable anti-ageing powerhouse!

TIPS TO HELP

- Breathe gently through your nose during this technique.
- Lightheadedness is to be expected in the beginning.
  Take a break if necessary.
- This is a great technique to use before and after exercise, when you wake up and before going to bed.

THE BREATH

Breathing only through your nose, jump up and down for at least one minute, and up to three minutes depending on your fitness. Let your calves power the movement while using the bounce to shed tension held in your body.

Come back to standing. Once your breathing has returned to normal, reach both arms upwards. Side bend over to the left and then to the right. Take a few deep breaths in each position to expand and stretch your sides. Let your arms relax and return to a neutral position.

PREVIOUS PAGE

Use your next few breaths to roll your upper body downwards, vertebra by vertebra, until your fingers drape on the floor (or as far as you can). Imagine each joint in your spine to articulate, one after the other.

Hanging upside down, focus on spreading your feet on the floor and sending your breath along the entire length of your spine: from neck to tailbone. Notice how each exhale helps to shed yet more body-held tension.

After thirty seconds of spinal breathing, rearticulate back up to standing.

Let your balance return before repeating the bounce and spinal articulation.

RIGHT

Afterwards, sit comfortably on the floor or a chair and, starting two inches below your navel, massage the lower abdomen in a clockwise direction.

Returning palms to belly, experiment by breathing into your palms again. How does it feel compared to when you first began?

Continue breathing this way for five minutes, using your exhale to release any remaining tension.

18. BREATH TO RELEASE ADDICTION

Ten Second Meditation

____

One of the challenges of addiction is how it impacts our whole being; an intense experience that overwhelms not only how we think and feel but the way we interpret things too. Breathing techniques are well suited to counter addiction due to their ability to stimulate our senses and encourage new behaviour. At first glance, *Ten Second Meditation* offers a momentary distraction but, in time and with practise, it helps to unpick the overactive pathways that keep us bound to the intensity of our inner experience.

The brain and body continually receive, interpret and make conclusions about the world around us; everything we encounter has impact. Our experience of these external stimuli would be meaningless but for how they are pieced together and defined by our mind and body. Using a complex framework of emotions and context, we usually interpret things as positive, neutral or negative; based on this, we either seek out the stimulation again, or make efforts to avoid it. *Ten Second Meditation* works by creating a wall of impact; a positive and conscious internal experience that can influence our whole body, dampening or evening out the negative signals that may be present. Though each cycle is short, when engaged in succession one after the other, this breath offers increasing lengths of respite by detaching us from what was originally attracting our attention. Breath has proven itself to be able to combat many types of addiction by helping us to cope with impulsivity, cravings and elements of associated stress and anxiety.

TIPS TO HELP

- Choose to breathe through either your mouth or nose. Stick to your choice. Committing in this way helps to develop focus; an essential quality to overcome addiction.

- Each time you engage this technique, notice how its impact strengthens. Tune into this intensity; it will help you work out how long to engage and how many repetitions you may need. We are all different.

- If you feel uncomfortably lightheaded, take a break. Consider slowing your breathing. Once feeling back to normal, try again. With practise, our body becomes less impacted by these sensations and, in the process, learns how to engage this technique more effectively.

THE BREATH

Breathe gently in any position to begin. Imagine each exhale to clear stagnant air from your body. Repeat for one minute.

After this minute, begin to inhale and exhale rapidly for ten seconds. Let your breathing be intense. Focus your mind on the sensations that arise from breathing this way. Return to normal breathing after ten seconds.

Observe your body; what do you notice?
Which areas were impacted?

Repeat another two ten-second cycles of this breath.

At the end of each cycle, re-scan your body.
Is there anything interesting that you notice?

Rest for at least one minute before finishing with two minutes of relaxed belly breathing.

Repeat as necessary.

19. BREATH FOR HEARTBURN

Diaphragmatic Breathing

———

Acid reflux is caused when the muscle that separates the stomach from the oesophagus allows acid from the stomach to rise upwards. Since the lining of our throat is sensitive, it becomes inflamed. Perhaps the greatest challenge of acid reflux is the variety of triggers that cause symptoms. These range from diet changes, sedentary lifestyles, and age. Breathing is helpful because we can calm our internal systems and restore natural body function.

The diaphragm plays a complex and under-researched role in its connection to acid reflux. Physiologically, we know the oesophagus penetrates the diaphragm through a hole called the hiatus. There is a ring of muscle located adjacent to this which is thought to be responsible for preventing contents of the stomach from coming back up the throat. Since the diaphragm is intimately connected to the throat, dysfunction and restriction can easily impact the whole digestive system.

Improving breathing movement and relieving tension stimulates a gentle internal massage of the whole abdominal area, while also restoring the parasympathetic nervous system. Practised on a daily basis, this technique creates a positive feedback loop: digestive rhythms are optimised, cravings balanced and healthier, or less aggravating, diet decisions can be more easily made.

TIPS TO HELP

- Ensure your knees are lower than your hips to help relax the lower abdomen.
- Try using segmental relaxation. Focus on releasing individual parts of your body during exhalation.

THE BREATH

Find yourself seated comfortably on a chair or sofa.

Place both hands on the lower abdomen, two inches below the belly button. Shut your eyes and begin to breathe in through the nose and out through the mouth.

Focusing on your palms, inhale slowly towards their position. Let your breath be full but relaxed.

Allowing a pause at the top of the breath, begin to exhale. Let it be effortless. Feel how your whole body can surrender and be held up by the chair underneath you.

Take another slow and full inhale. Give time for your breath to fill your palms.

Allow another pause at the top of the breath before exhaling.

Continue breathing this way for fifteen to twenty minutes.

For best results, complete the breath half an hour before eating, or whenever you feel heartburn.

20. BREATH TO IMPROVE POSTURE

The Star

————

From the perspective of posture, the way we live and how we design our living spaces is, quite literally, terrifying. It is as though we are hell-bent on a lifestyle, including the use of furniture and technology, that mocks the inherent workings and functions of our body. The conflict starts early too: we are not designed to sit as much as we do; we are not designed to engage in repetitive and imbalanced exercise as much as we do; many of the technologies designed to make our lives easier only aggravate and detract from our well-being.

Our spine begins to deteriorate from as young as our early twenties: the space in between each vertebra compresses, joints stiffen and dehydrate and important minerals leach from our bones. *The Star* helps to counter these by developing a strong, flexible corset of muscles around the spine, ribs and back.

By maintaining the health of these important joints, it is possible to safeguard our posture no matter our age. *The Star* is an essential breath for helping to boost circulation, improve digestion, and naturally resolve any musculoskeletal imbalance.

TIPS TO HELP

- The shape and size of one's buttocks in relation to our shoulders can make spinal alignment difficult. If you have strong curves in your spine, use a pole, rather than a wall, to encourage more length between each vertebra.
- If your natural head position is forwards, prop a book or firm pillow behind your head. The need for such props will diminish with practise over time.
- Throughout the exercise, focus on broadening your chest and shoulders.

THE BREATH

Stand with your back against a wall with palms facing forwards.

Move your heels ten to fifteen centimetres away from the wall, seeking to align your buttocks and the back of your head flat against the surface behind you.

Take a deep inhale. Feel how breathing in naturally lengthens your spine and neck.

Engaging your legs, standing strong and tall, start to breathe out. Use the muscular contractions of the exhale to stretch (rather than compress) your spine. Feel how your abdominal muscles work like a corset. Let them lift and lengthen.

Hold the breath out for a few seconds. Double efforts to lengthen your spine as you press your buttocks and head backwards, firmly. Return to natural breathing when you need.

Imagining your spine is able to stretch even longer, on your next inhale, stretch your arms out wide and press them backwards.

During exhalation, see how flat you can press them against the wall.

Return to natural breathing, experimenting with moving your arms like angel wings against the wall: upwards during exhalation and downwards on inhalation

Repeat three cycles of each twice daily.
Add cycles during periods of prolonged sitting.

21. BREATH TO SURVIVE LONGER UNDERWATER

The Dive

_____

From the youngest age, I remember enjoying breath-holding; in hindsight, it was not the safest pastime for a four-year-old to be practising in the local splash pool. Today, breath-holding captivates millions of children and adults alike. David Blaine was perhaps the first to attract large-scale interest through a live performance of breath control on *The Oprah Winfrey Show* in 2008, where he smashed all breath-holding records with a whopping time of seventeen minutes and four seconds. This record has been broken a number of times since then, the current record holder being Aleix Segura Vendrell with a time of twenty-four minutes and three seconds.

When we hold our breath and feel that building desire to breathe, it is easy to mistake the discomfort for a sign that we are running out of oxygen. In fact, the diaphragmatic spasms, burning chest and rush of feelings of impending doom highlight something completely different: that our body has noticed carbon dioxide levels are rising. This is interesting because, since it is oxygen we need to survive, it would be possible to ignore these intense spasms to breathe for at least another minute or so before putting ourselves in any real danger. As a result, it is possible to train our body to handle greater levels of carbon dioxide. *The Dive* teaches us to do this safely. It also redirects peripheral blood supply to important organs and slows down our heartbeat. With practise, not only do we feel able to hold our breath for longer, but we stimulate the production of red blood cells. This further helps our body to become more efficient, requiring less effort from the heart and lungs for the same output. This technique is adapted from what the free-diving world describes as working CO_2 tables.

TIPS TO HELP

- Take your time. Work to a level that challenges rather than hurts you.
- Engage exercises safely, away from water or dangerous machinery.
- Practise with a friend or connect with a local freediving club.

THE BREATH

First, we need to work out your baseline. This is the length of time you can easily hold your breath to. To find this out, sit in a relaxed position and breathe naturally for one minute.

At the end of this minute, inhale to fifty percent of your capacity and hold your breath. Use a stopwatch to measure the length of time it takes for you to crave your next breath.

Test yourself another two times, ensuring you take a minute break between each test.

Calculate your average time and note this down. This is your level 1 baseline.

Next, breathe naturally for fifty seconds. Inhale to fifty percent of your capacity and, using the stopwatch, hold your breath for the length of your level 1 baseline.

Repeat this process another four times, reducing the length of time you rest in between breath-holds by ten-second increments. This means your final round of natural breathing will be for ten seconds before re-holding your breath.

Return to natural breathing. Practise regularly for best results.

To develop this breath: at the end of the first week, add five seconds to your level 1 baseline. This becomes level 2. Each week, add another five seconds to your baseline to become level 3, level 4, etc.

Where to Next?

Have you ever sat on a beach and wondered, "Where would I end up if I just kept swimming?" I like to imagine the exotic beaches and wild adventures waiting over the horizon. Sadly, I realise such a journey will forever be out of my reach. Other than for the few already committed to a lifetime of training, it would be too hard and too dangerous for most of us to swim so far.

Similarly, I find myself wondering about breath, too. I love to imagine the journeys we could travel and the opportunities that lay in our path should we explore breathing beyond how we usually breathe. Compared to marathon swimming, though, breath is different. With breath, we are already very capable and have already effortlessly completed a lifetime of training. In fact, if we could swim as naturally as we breathed, we would all be world-class endurance athletes. Imagine only just finding this out... it would be like waking up on an tropical beach and realising you had swum all the way there!

Beyond writing about the extraordinary capabilities of breath, the intention of this book has been to show that you *are* already capable; that you *can* already access wherever you want within your own world of breath.

I wonder where your breath will take you next?

RECOMMENDED READING

Beachy, Will, *Respiratory Care Anatomy and Physiology: Foundations for Clinical Practice*, 4th Edition. Elsevier, 2018.

Bostok, Richie, *Exhale: How to Use Breathwork to Find Calm, Supercharge Your Health and Perform at Your Best*. Penguin Life, 2020.

Brown, Dr. Richard P. and Gerbarg, Dr. Patricia, *The Healing Power of the Breath: Simple Techniques to Reduce Stress and Anxiety, Enhance Concentration, and Balance Your Emotions*. Shambala, 2012.

Brule, Dan, *Just Breathe: Mastering Breathwork*. Enliven Books, 2020.

Carney, Scott, *What Doesn't Kill Us: the bestselling guide to transforming your body by unlocking your lost evolutionary strength*. Scribe, 2019.

Farhi, Donna, *The Breathing Book: Vitality and Good Health Through Essential Breath Work*. Henry Holt, 1996.

Givens, Jerry, *Essential Pranayama: Breathing Techniques for Balance, Healing, and Peace*. Rockridge Press, 2020.

Grof, Stanislav and Grof, Christina, *Holotropic Breathwork: A New Approach to Self-Exploration and Therapy*. Excelsior Editions, 2010.

Hall, Jean, *Breathe: simple breathing techniques for a calmer, happier life*. Quadrille Publishing, 2016.

Hartley, Aimee, *Breathe Well: Easy and effective exercises to boost energy, feel calmer, more focused and productive*. Kyle Books, 2020.

Hendricks, Gay, *Conscious Breathing: Breathwork for Health, Stress Release and Personal Mastery*. Bantam, 1997.

Hof, Wim, *The Wim Hof Method: Activate Your Potential, Transcend Your Limits*. Rider, 2020.

Kravitz, Judith, *Breathe Deep, Laugh Loudly: The Joy of Transformational Breathing*. Ini Freepress, 1999.

McKeown, Patrick, *The Oxygen Advantage*. Piatkus, 2015.

Morningstar, Jim, *Break Through with Breathwork: Jump-Starting Personal Growth in Counselling and the Healing Arts*. North Atlantic Books, 2017.

Moselle, Valerie, *Breathwork: A 3-Week Breathing Program to Gain Clarity, Calm, and Better Health*. Althea Press, 2019.

Neese, Ashley, *How to Breathe: 25 Simple Practices for Calm, Joy, and Resilience*. September Publishing, 2019.

Nestor, James, *Breath: The New Science of a Lost Art*. Penguin Life, 2020.

Olsson, Anders, *Conscious Breathing: Discover the Power of Your Breath*. Sorena AB, 2014.

Penman, Dr. Danny, *The Art of Breathing: The secret to living mindfully. Just don't breath a word of it*. Conari Press, 2018.

Saradananda, Swami. *The Power of Breath: Yoga Breathing for Inner Balance, Health and Harmony*. Watkins, 2009.

Smart, Andrew, *Breathwork: How to Use Your Breath to Change Your Life (Breathing Techniques for Anxiety Relief and Stress, Breath Exercises for Mindfulness and Self-Care)*. Chronicle Books, 2020.

Sneider, Lutz, *The Power of Breathing Techniques: Breathing Exercises for more Fitness, Health and Relaxation*. Expertengruppe, 2019.

Timmermans, Anna, *Beyond Defense: Core Energetic Techniques*. 2018.

Tonkov, Giten, *Feel to Heal: Releasing Trauma Through Body Awareness and Breathwork Practice*. Biodynamic Breathwork & Trauma Release Institute, 2019.

Tudor, Una. *The Little Book of Breathing: Simple practices for connecting with your breath*. Gaia, 2019.

Vranich, Dr. Belisa and Saben, Brian, *Breathing for Warriors: Master Your Breath to Unlock More Strength, Greater Endurance, Sharper Precision, Faster Recovery, and an Unshakable Inner Game*. St. Martin's Essentials, 2020.

Werner, Dylan, *The Illuminated Breath: Transform Your Physical, Cognitive & Emotional Well-Being by Harnessing the Science of Ancient Yoga Breath Practices*. Victory Belt, 2021.

Westmacott-Brown, Nathalia, *Breathwork: Use the Power of Breath to Energise Your Body and Focus Your Mind (A Little Book of Self Care)*. DK, 2019.

For a full bibliography visit the *21 Breaths* page at www.worldofbreath.com

To my family, friends and everyone who I have had, and will ever have, the privilege of sharing breath with. You are the best teachers.

Ian, Katie, Lauren, Felicity and the Unicorn Publishing team, thank you for believing.

And dearest Buket and Dari, my breath will catch on your beautiful work for ever.

ABOUT THE AUTHOR

 Oliver first connected with breath through pain; from the age of twenty-one he experienced chronic and debilitating lower back pain that, over a two-year period, spread rapidly throughout his whole body. Despite receiving some of the best medical treatment, Oliver's pain only seemed to increase. Hitting rock bottom in 2004, he felt he had no choice but to explore alternative options. Within five years, and over two hundred alternative practices experienced, not only had Oliver recovered but he felt fitter and healthier than he ever had before. Throughout this journey back to health, he noticed breath played an important role in almost every one of these alternative practices. Inspired into action, Oliver connected with pioneers of body psychotherapy, movement, massage and breathwork from around the world. Today, he supports others to experience for themselves the self-empowering, restorative capabilities held in their breath.